UNIVERSITY LIBRARY
UNIVERSITY OF ILLINOIS AT URBANA

...ing this material is responsible for its
...ry on or before the due date.

...? for

W9-DJE-401

SUPER KIDS

ORDINARY KIDS WHO HAVE DONE
EXTRAORDINARY THINGS

WITHDRAWN
University of
Illinois Library
at Urbana-Champaign

SUPER KIDS

ORDINARY KIDS WHO HAVE DONE EXTRAORDINARY THINGS

by Lisa Fitterman
Illustrated by Caren Scarpulla

HYLAS
PUBLISHING

HYLAS
PUBLISHING

Hylas Publishing
129 Main Street
Irvington, New York 10533
www.hylaspublishing.com

Text and illustrations copyright © 2005 Hylas Publishing
All rights reserved under International and Pan-American Copyright Conventions.
No part of this publication may be reproduced, stored in a retrieval system, or
transmitted in any form or by any means, electronic, mechanical, photocopying,
recording or otherwise, without the prior written permission of the copyright owner.

Hylas Publishing
Publisher: Sean Moore
Creative Director: Karen Prince
Art Directors: Edwin Kuo, Gus Yoo
Editorial Director: Lori Baird
Production Manager: Sarah Reilly

Project Credits
Editor(s): Suzanne Lander, Matt Silverman
Assistant/Associate Editor: Angda Goel
Project Editor: Gail Greiner
Jacket Design and Illustration: Caren Scarpulla
Interior Design: La Tricia Watford, Rachel Maloney, Kathleen Massaro, Gavin Motnyk

Fitterman, Lisa.
Super kids: ordinary kids who have done extraordinary things / by Lisa Fitterman;
illustrated by Caren Scarpulla.—1st American ed. p. cm.
ISBN 1-59258-136-6
1. Children—Biography—Juvenile literature. 2. Biography—Juvenile literature.
I. Scarpulla, Caren. II. Title.
CT107.F525 2005
305.23'092'273—dc22
2005018567

Printed and bound in the USA
Distributed by National Book Network
First American Edition published in 2005
1 3 5 7 9 10 8 6 4 2

S.305.23092273
F56ls
cop.2

S.Coll.
(Educ.)

To Sam and Fanny,
the superkids in my life.
—*L. F.*

⊂ CONTENTS ∾

INTRODUCTION

"Kids do the darndest things," or so the saying goes. This book signals a real change, because lots of kids do really amazing things—so many, in fact, that only a few dozen of them could be included in this book.

It's always the hardest part of writing: to cut something down to the right size. That was especially true in this case. Where there is one brave child, there could have been 50 or 100 or 1,000. The same goes for musicians, community activists, athletes, or the courageous kids who manage to keep a positive outlook even when confronted with catastrophic illnesses such as AIDS or cancer.

They're all impressive both individually and taken as a whole. One could even make the argument that all kids are heroes or at least have the potential to be. Most of the great kids portrayed in Super Kids don't have extraordinary strength or super-genius brains. Rather, they are just like you. They go to school, skateboard or ski, and they hang with friends. The difference, if there is one, is that they had an idea and ran with it, or they maintained their cool in a moment of crisis and helped save others—even as their world was literally falling apart all around them.

What this exceptional group of young people all have

in common is that they rose up in response to their specific circumstances, no matter if they live in a tiny village in western Africa; St. Louis, Missouri; a suburb in Australia; or on a Mohawk reserve in Quebec, Canada.

Indeed, it has been said that the strength of a country can be measured by what happens on Main Street—in schools and where ordinary people live and work. Given the impressive evidence that we found while doing the research for this book, the future will be safe in the extremely capable and caring hands of the next generation.

As David Adamiec, one of the boys profiled here, said, "It gets me that grown-ups write us off as troublemakers. We're not, and if I can change one adult's mind over what kids are about, then that's just fine with me."

Don't read these stories and think: "I could never do that." Choose, instead, to be inspired, for you don't know what you can do—and you'll never know until you just do it.

There's an ancient Chinese proverb that goes: "A journey of a thousand miles begins with a single step."

So rise up. Be in control. Help others. Lead.

～1～
TO THE RESCUE!

Sometimes, kids can surprise you with their knowledge, their bravery, and their willingness to go one or six extra steps to make sure that everyone is okay. In this chapter, some kids were heroes for knowing when to get out. Others acted with extraordinary bravery in the face of life-threatening incidents or, in the case of one young Florida boy, the unexpected birth of his baby sister!

Bikes and Bandages

Andy Morrison and his friends loved racing their bikes down the steep blacktop surface of Embassy Drive in Charleston, West Virginia. They'd do it over and over, screeching tires around a big curve before coming to the end.

One day, though, things didn't go quite as planned. That afternoon, Andy's friend Will Smoot missed the curve and went flying off his bike! He smashed into a utility pole's wires and then kept going, finally landing on a narrow creek bank about fifty feet below the road.

Andy and the others watched, horrified, as their friend fell. They flinched when his right leg hit the ground so hard that his foot was partly torn from his ankle. The long bones that extended from his knee were buried in the muck. There was blood everywhere, gushing from Will's leg and foot.

Most of the boys panicked and sped off, but twelve-year-old Andy, a longtime Scout, couldn't go. Boy Scout training had taught him that Will would go into shock and maybe even bleed to death, and Andy couldn't let that happen.

He wrapped a towel around the injured boy's leg, tying it as tight as he could. Ever so slowly, the flow of blood slowed down. Andy stayed with his friend until help arrived.

For saving Will's life, Andy was awarded a Boy Scouts' hero's medal—although he said he was scared half to death at the time and hadn't felt brave at all.

How Paying Attention in Class Could Save Your Life

(and Others', Too)

Tilly Smith knew exactly what was going on when the water on the beach bubbled, then disappeared. As other tourists on Maikhao Beach in Phuket, Thailand, marveled at the stranded, flopping fish, the ten-year-old remained calm as she firmly said, "Mummy, we must get off the beach now."

Only a few weeks earlier, Tilly had completed a project about tsunamis at her school in Oxshott, England—and she recalled what she had learned there. She knew that the suddenly vanished water meant that there had been an earthquake somewhere beneath the sea. This meant that the ocean was gathering up all its strength before unleashing it back on to the land through a series of giant and deadly waves.

She clearly remembered the video in geography class in which a survivor described a tsunami. The water got sucked away, then came hurtling back minutes later, crashing, smashing, and destroying everything in its path. So she knew that there was no time to waste. Everyone around her had no more than ten minutes to get off the beach and onto higher ground if they had any chance of escaping safely.

Tilly's parents, instead of dismissing her as just a child with an overactive imagination, took her very seriously indeed. They raced to warn other people on the beach and in the hotel. Minutes after the area was evacuated, a huge wave crashed over the sands, sweeping away everything before it.

Tilly's mother, Penny, said that at first, she'd simply wanted to stare like everyone else at the sudden, unexpected expanse of sand and the stranded fish.

"But when Tilly explained what was going to happen, I had second thoughts," she explained. "We ran off the beach as fast as we could. I dread to think what would have happened if we had stayed."

Thanks to Tilly, her beach was one of the few in Phuket where no one was killed or even badly injured! Everyone called her a hero—except, of course, shy Tilly herself.

Give Me a Brake

ᴗᴄᴗᴄᴗᴄᴗᴄᴗᴄᴗᴄᴗᴄᴗᴄ

Imagine you're on a runaway school bus on an interstate highway, with the lone adult lying crumpled in the exit stairwell, and all the kids are screaming bloody murder. What in the world are you going to do?

Young Larry Champagne knew this: He sure wasn't going to let anyone die—not if he could help it.

Luckily ten-year-old Larry had been taught to drive, sort of, by his grandfather. They'd go up and down the driveway of the man's home, braking and accelerating slightly as the boy got comfortable behind the wheel.

As part of a voluntary program that mixed kids up by neighborhood, Larry and his brother went to a school twenty miles away from their home in St. Louis, Missouri. Their bus was traveling on busy U.S. Highway 40 when Ernestine Blackman, the driver, suddenly gasped and collapsed. There was silence for a moment, and then the twenty other student passengers, including Larry's brother, began to scream and cry. Larry knew that something had to be done, so he remained calm and began to act.

The whole situation reminded Larry of the movie *Speed*, in which a runaway bus was wired to explode if it slowed down. Like the character in the movie, Larry knew he had to be brave and do something about this bad real-life situation. So he got up from his seat, marched to the front of the bus, took the wheel, and pressed his foot on the brake.

There were a few bumps and small crashes along the way. The bus did hit some guardrails before it stopped. Then a truck driver, not realizing that the bus had been out of control in the first place, struck them from behind. Thankfully, nobody was injured. Larry had saved the day.

It turned out that the driver had had a stroke, so an ambulance arrived and took her to a hospital. The police came, too, as well as a new bus to pick up the kids, who kept chanting, "Larry saved our lives. Larry saved our lives."

Larry didn't really understand why his actions were such a big deal. After all, he had done only what he had to so that everyone would survive.

Call 9-1-1!

ᴗᴄᴧᴗᴄᴧᴗᴄᴧᴗᴄᴧᴗᴄᴧᴄᴧᴗᴄᴧ

Christopher Fyfe was just learning how to ride a bicycle when he came to his mother's rescue. The four-year-old boy from Calgary, Alberta, was waiting for his breakfast when his mom had a seizure and collapsed right in front of him.

Other kids might have panicked, but Christopher didn't hesitate for a second. His dad had taught him how to get help, so he went to the phone, dialed 9-1-1, and told the dispatcher, "My mom's wiggling."

The dispatcher, Richard Agnew, had no idea Christopher was only four. How could he? The little boy sounded calm and mature as he provided information, checked his mom's breathing, made sure she hadn't bitten her tongue, and said, "I'm really worried about her."

By the time paramedics got to the house, his mom had regained consciousness. She saw her son on the phone and took the receiver. "What number is this?" she asked, woozy and completely unaware of what had just happened.

Christopher knew he'd done a good thing. Clutching a stuffed moose he'd gotten for his bravery, he told reporters, "I'm a smart boy."

9·1·1

16

A Heimlich Hug

At a Red Cross training session, ten-year-old Brad DalSanto learned the Heimlich maneuver. He loved that it looked like a bear hug from behind, but was meant to stop someone from choking to death. Little did the boy from South Beloit, Illinois, know that only ten days after learning it, he'd use the Heimlich to save his sister's life!

It happened on Super Bowl Sunday. Seven-year-old Becky was chewing on a plastic quarter when she began to gag. The quarter was stuck in her throat! She ran into the family room, where her mother and brother were watching the game. Both realized she was choking, and her mom began to hit her back, but that didn't help.

Then Brad calmly got behind his sister, wrapped his arms around her in that Heimlich bear hug, thrust in and up with his hands, and *poof!* The quarter popped out. "After that, we threw out the coin and all the others," he said.

For his quick thinking, Brad got an American Red Cross Award for Extraordinary Personal Action, was chosen as a local radio personality's kid of the week. He was also named a real live hero by Hasbro, which makes the G.I. Joe action figure, for saving his little sister's life.

As for Becky, she got a lot of relieved hugs. Then her mom lectured her for putting that quarter in her mouth in the first place, which she knew she shouldn't have done.

OH, BROTHER

ᔕᏨᎪᔕᏨᎪᔕᏨᎪᔕᏨᎪᔕᏨᎪᎪᔕᏨᎪ

Clarence Woods will never forget the day he got an unexpected crash course in where babies come from. In fact, it was the day he helped deliver his little sister.

Eight-year-old Clarence was alone with their mother in their Orlando, Florida, home while his four younger siblings were being taken to the babysitter's. The baby wasn't due for another month, but Vervicia Woods had had a few pains the night before and was headed for the hospital once the baby's father got back from dropping off the kids. Clarence had stayed with her—just in case.

Just in case turned into just right then and there. His mother's pains got worse—very fast. When her water broke (a sign that the baby was coming really soon), she collapsed. She wasn't even able to reach the phone let alone get to the hospital. So quick-thinking Clarence remained calm and asked: "Now, should I call nine-one-one?"

"Uh-huh," his mother replied, gritting her teeth. Clarence dialed 9-1-1 at 9:23 a.m., and for the next five minutes, dispatcher Maureen Grether stayed on the line with him, talking him through the delivery.

Clarence ran back and forth between the phone, which wasn't portable, and his mom, relaying instructions and answering questions. He told his mom to breathe in, one-two-three-four, and out, one-two-three-four.

At one point—it seemed like forever—he told the dispatcher the baby's head was out.

She told Clarence to have his mom push, push really hard to get the rest of the baby out. And when his sister finally emerged, he made sure she was breathing properly.

At this point, the paramedics arrived, cut the umbilical cord, and rushed them all to the hospital. Thanks to Clarence, Jessica Joanne Ashley was just fine!

And what did he think of seeing his sister come out of his mom's body?

"It was okay," he said, wrinkling his nose.

Snow Survivor

It was supposed to be a simple trip from their home near Montreal, Quebec, to their cozy cottage up north. In March 2003, eleven-year-old Leia Hunt and her dad, David, set off on their snowmobile ride without a care in the world. At first, everything was fine—the weather was mild and they were making good time. After they'd traveled about sixty-five miles, though, their world turned upside down. The snowmobile flipped over a drainpipe and crashed down a ravine in the middle of the Canadian wilderness!

Leia's dad couldn't walk because his knee had been smashed during the accident. So, after the two of them spent the night huddled together in the bitter cold that dropped to minus-22 degrees Fahrenheit, Leia went by herself to find

help. She struggled for two miles, braving howling winds and lurking hungry wolves before she came to a small community they'd passed the day before on the snowmobile. A search party had been called out to look for the missing snowmobilers, and Leia told them where her dad was.

Later, she would remember the storekeeper who did his best to comfort her with chocolate chip cookies as the rescuers tried to get her boots off. Her feet were frozen solid. It took twenty minutes just to remove the boot on her left foot. Unfortunately, her right leg was such a block of ice that it had to be soaked in water for half an hour before her foot would even come out of the boot! Even while her feet were thawing out, which was really throbbing and painful, Leia was glad she had made that difficult journey so that her father could get rescued.

"I wasn't just going to sit around and watch my dad be in pain," she said of her ordeal.

Because of frostbite, doctors had to cut off most of her right foot as well as the toes on her left.

Since then, Leia hasn't let her handicap stop her. She loves to swim and even as she does laps in her grandmother's pool, she dreams of the day when she will swim with dolphins, her favorite creatures in the world.

Pulled Out
of the Fire

Early one autumn morning, after his dad had already gone to work, a propane explosion jolted ten-year-old Alex Wickenkamp straight out of bed. He raced to get his family out of their home in Oskaloosa, Iowa. It wasn't easy.

First, he literally pushed his big sister, Jessica, in shock in her basement bedroom, up to the main floor. A few minutes later, an explosion engulfed the basement in flames.

Alex pulled his four-year-old brother Evan out next. Trapped in her bedroom, Alex's mom, Tami, heard Alex's voice and found the strength to push the collapsed headboard off her body. The mother and her children were together, yet still far from safe. The front door was blocked! Alex led everyone through the kitchen then jumped down into the yard to race to safety. His mom could see Jessica and Evan, but where was Alex? She called and called and suddenly, there he was, under a neighbor's tree—the spot the family had planned as a meeting place in case of an emergency!

CaNDY FiRST AiD

When elderly Atanacio Lehija shouted that his five-year-old grandson was choking on a piece of candy and turning blue from lack of oxygen, Ashly Saleen knew exactly what to do.

Ashly, twelve, who had been hanging out nearby with some kids in her Patterson, California, neighborhood, very calmly laid Joey De La Cruz across her lap and, with the heel of her hand, pushed hard several times between his shoulder blades. Within seconds, she managed to dislodge the candy. The boy could breathe again, and she was hailed as a hero.

Ashly had known just what to do for Joey because she was one of the first in her neighborhood to take a CPR, or cardio-pulmonary resuscitation, life-saving course offered by the local fire department. She'd wanted to be prepared just in case something terrible happened to any of the kids she would babysit—something exactly like this!

It certainly was a class worth taking.

"Joey got up and started playing and running around again, so I didn't think much more about it," she said. "It felt good, but I sure hope I never have to do something like that again." Even so, Ashly will be prepared—just in case.

It's good that Ashly got to take the CPR course in the first place. The fire department staff had thought that the twelve-year-old might be too young, but she's proof that knowledge, not age, matters when it comes to saving lives.

৩2৯
SMARTIES

Yes, some kids are simply born brilliant. You can't get away from it. Try to imagine, though, the difficulties they have balancing their lives. Some are mere kids while they attend some of the world's most prestigious universities. Others must overcome hurdles like lack of money or having to learn a new language. Just close your eyes and imagine it's your first day of school in a new country, you speak very little of the language, and no one is talking to you.

Bachar, the Brain

When Canadians talk of a brain drain to the United States, usually they're referring to the best and brightest adults who find better opportunities south of the border. Preschoolers don't normally figure into the discussion.

Bachar Sbeiti was only three when he was sent to the Roeper School for gifted students in Bloomfield Hills, Michigan. He can name the capital of any country in three languages: English, French, and Arabic.

Uzbekistan? *Tashkent.* Fiji? *Suva.*

People couldn't help but notice that little Bachar never forgot a thing. Bachar's mom didn't have the money to send her son to a special private school. Bachar, though supersmart, would have had to wait two years, until he turned five, to go to a public school in Canada.

In stepped the National Association of Arab Americans in Detroit, which raised $24,000—enough for two years at Roeper. The NAAA members were amazed that Bachar could recite the ninety-nine names given to God in Islam and in the right order. Why, they were adults and couldn't recall five in the right order, never mind all ninety-nine!

Until he goes to school in Canada, he'll be studying his ABC's and capital cities in the U.S. He sighs when asked the capital of the country where he goes to school. *What a no-brainer*, he implies. It's Washington, D.C.—of course!

SeaRCHiNG FOR a CURe

At first glance, Masoud Karkehabadi didn't seem all that different than most other kids his age. He skateboarded and played street hockey, and his parents always made sure he was in bed by 10 p.m. at the very latest! Masoud had one interest, though, that most kids didn't have—he wanted to discover a cure for Parkinson's disease.

Young Masoud never went to school until he entered college—at age nine. The mastermind from Mission Viejo, California, was schooled at home until he was accepted at the University of California, Irvine. There, he devoted himself to his studies, going to classes, operating on rats, and, under the supervision of a neuroscience professor, looking for a way to stop brain cells from dying. His goal was to find a cure for Parkinson's disease.

Masoud had developed an early interest in this terrible disease after reading about it in medical journals. He learned that people who suffer from Parkinson's find it harder and harder to control their movements until, one day, they are no longer able to move at all.

Through this concerned interest, the California college kid became a pint-sized spokesperson for the American Parkinson's Disease Association. He traveled around the country, appearing on talk shows, giving newspaper interviews, and generally appearing thoughtful on a subject that most people his age had no idea even existed. At age thirteen, Masoud became his school's youngest graduate.

He presented his research to a group of doctors in Portland, Oregon. Several television documentaries even featured Masoud and his dedication to finding a cure.

How, people asked, could someone so young be so composed, bright, and driven?

"I believe my intelligence is a gift from God," Masoud once said. "I want to use it to the best of my capacity to help society." So Masoud continues his research, doing his part to try to make a better world.

WORD BUILDER

Katie Devanney is a P-R-O-D-I-G-Y at Scrabble. This kid from Villanova, Pennsylvania, has been beating adult players, one after another, since she began competing at age twelve.

Katie travels to tournaments, learning to strategize and building on previous experience as she chalks up wins. Usually the youngest player, she frequently ends up doing much better than her more experienced competitors.

The seventh-grader has a National Scrabble Association rating of 1,011, putting her in the upper level of novice class. When—not if—she gets a 1,200 rating (something adult players can struggle for years to earn), this talented teen will be playing on a near-expert level. Why, she has even beaten Jan Dixon, one of the world's top-ranked women players!

"I've always loved words," Katie said, "and I love to write and read, so Scrabble kind of fits in that category." Her favorite subject is science, and she wants to be a doctor. For now, though, she's only too happy to concentrate on words and strategy.

What does B-R-I-L-L-I-A-N-T spell? Katie not only knows, she can even turn it into a triple-word score in Scrabble.

Making the Code

One of the most famous secret messages in the history of codes is: "June 6 Invasion: Normandy." *D-Day*. On this day in 1944, Allied forces stormed the shores of Normandy, France, during World War II. It's also the message that Viviana Risca hid in a strand of DNA when she was a high school student in Port Washington, New York.

Viviana won the Intel Science Talent Search with the project and was awarded a $100,000 scholarship. She had managed this after emigrating with her family from Romania when she was in third grade. Then the Romanian girl couldn't speak English, except for phrases such as "Where is the bathroom?" and "How do I get home?"

It was lonely at first, but she found refuge in subjects like math and science. She was good at it and worked very hard. So when her high school teacher proposed the DNA project, Viviana leaped at the opportunity.

After she won the Intel contest, Viviana shared the podium at a DNA seminar with Nobel Laureate James Watson, a genetics pioneer, and co-wrote a scientific paper on DNA encryption that was published in the journal *Nature*.

Only a few years earlier, she would have barely been able to ask directions to a newsstand to buy a copy of the journal. Viviana's accomplishments show that hard work and commitment can sometimes bring incredible results.

A Real-Life Kid Doc

vɔenvɔenvɔenvɔenvɔenenvɔen

Sho Yano can remember the day that he decided to be a doctor. It happened one Christmas morning after he had gotten a human anatomy coloring book as one of his presents. He had been three years old at the time.

Less than a decade later, he was at his first day of classes at the University of Chicago's medical school. He was twelve. Though he was a bit uncomfortable with the idea of having to cut up a dead body, it wasn't something any of the other medical students were really thrilled about either. In fact, many of his much older classmates took that particular assignment much harder than he did!

With an I.Q. of 200, he'd always been great at science, math, and music. However, his young age raised lots of questions. How old, or young, should one be to study medicine or attend any kind of university, for that matter? Just how would Sho socialize with his classmates? Was he too young to withstand the stress of medical school?

He took all of the concerns and questions in stride. Sho already knew he was different and that some people might not understand him. Several medical schools had rejected his application because the admissions board thought that Sho was too young to attend. When the Pritzer School of

Medicine at the University of Chicago accepted him, it was with the condition that he could not treat live patients until he reached the ripe old age of seventeen!

Until that time, he had to work only with actors pretending to be ill. Yet, even though they were actors, Sho gave them his complete and total attention. Everybody agreed that he did a very good job of it; it seemed to come quite naturally to him. He expressed more concern and caring for these "patients" than many other aspiring doctors did who were old enough to work with the real thing.

Michelle LeBeau, head of the university's cancer biology program, said she was particularly impressed with his reply to a situation in which a very sick mother had just given birth to twins. Sho thought for a moment, then said, "She must be very scared." Such understanding and compassion will be a positive force in the future of medicine.

Eyes on the Prize

ↄↄ

Balmurali Ambati stood six feet tall on his first day at the Mount Sinai School of Medicine in New York City. It was a good thing, given that all the other students were on the lookout for the little fourteen-year-old kid they imagined would be running around in their midst.

"Even a month later, people would come up to me and ask, 'Have you met the fourteen-year-old yet?'" he once recalled with a shrug and a smile. "You get used to it. Your colleagues get used to it. Then it's not a big deal."

Balmurali, who had moved from India to New York when he was three, is used to being different. Even though he played basketball and Ping-Pong with friends his own age, he whizzed through school two grades a year. He then went on to college, where he completed his undergraduate degree in two years. After college came medical school, which took him a little while longer; he didn't graduate with a degree in medicine until he was seventeen!

Now an eye surgeon at the Medical College of Georgia, he decided to become a doctor when he saw a news story about a medical student in Israel who'd graduated at age eighteen. Well, Balmurali beat that person's pace by a year, and he was finished with his studies sooner than most of his fellow students, some who had maybe spent too much of their time looking for that fourteen-year-old kid.

FOOD FIGHT!

It was a great kid's computer game: talking vegetables and fruits with names like Tommy Tomato and Billy Banana, having a sticky, squishy food fight!

Sure, inventor Kevin Richard, of Saugus, Massachusetts, may have been in the second grade, but he had the confidence and sass of someone much older. "I'm seven," he told a magazine back when his computer game first hit the market. "When I'm not on the computer, I eat, watch TV, play Nintendo, blah blah blah. Just what you would expect. And I also have a sense of humor." For his cool game "Food Fight," the Boston Computer Society awarded Kevin with top honors in his age group. This was an improvement over the year before, when he'd taken third place.

Even at seven, Kevin was a budding entrepreneur. He started a company called Silly Software, fixed up an office in the family basement, and hired his dad to work for him. He decided not to hire his four-year-old brother Eddie, though, because the boy liked to scribble on everything and not act properly in general—kids!

~ 3 ~
STRENGTH IN THE FACE OF SICKNESS

Some of the kids in this chapter have faced down diseases such as AIDS, cancer, and diabetes, while others were born with serious conditions that could have made them outcasts. However, every single one responded to these incredible challenges in ways that affected the people around them positively. Read on.

A Kid Who Cares

Ian Amber was ten years old when he found out that he had cancer and knew his life would never be the same.

He put up with a lot—long weeks of chemotherapy, lying in bed with needles stuck in his arm as his body was bombarded with drugs to kill the cancer cells. Ian knew how hard it was to stay optimistic, with bad thoughts that snuck in screaming, "I'm going to die!" He figured there must be plenty of other kids in the same position.

So Ian, of Pinecrest, Florida, and his brother Kyle started the Kids That Care Pediatric and Cancer Fund. The idea was to make sure sick kids were surrounded by compassion and a sense of optimism. He wanted sick kids to feel that anything they put their minds to was possible, no matter how weak their bodies. A natural organizer, Ian learned how to do everything from writing grant applications to getting companies to donate prizes for charity raffles.

Each year, he organizes the Kids That Care Ouch Box Toy Drive. People and businesses donate toys to local hospitals so young patients can receive a gift every time they get a treatment. Ian knows what it can mean to take home something positive from an excruciating experience. "Through my work with Kids That Care," he wrote, "I have learned that I enjoy helping others and that it is rewarding to improve the lives of those with life-threatening illnesses."

ROLE MODEL

Never mind that Kim Beal had spent years fighting for her own life after contracting a rare form of cancer. What this young lady is most proud of is the time, when she was ten, that she saved the life of another girl.

Kim, of Addison, Maine, had traveled with her 4-H group to nearby Ellsworth to see a rabbit show. The hotel where they were staying had a sign near the pool that warned: "NO LIFEGUARD ON DUTY. NO CHILDREN IN POOL WITHOUT ADULT SUPERVISION."

Of course, there was one adult with the group was who watching the kids in the pool, but she was distracted at the exact same moment that four-year-old Morgan Beal (no relation to Kim) jumped into the water!

Kim looked back to see who'd made the big splash and saw a head bobbing up and down and lots of churning water. At first, she thought it was one of her friends, but she quickly realized it wasn't, and that the person didn't know how to swim. Kim jumped in, grabbed the little girl around her stomach, and got her to the edge of the pool. Morgan was panicking and grabbing onto Kim's neck, but the older girl stayed calm and didn't let go of her.

"I feel proud because I saved someone's life," she said. "It made me feel great inside. I still feel like a hero, I guess."

Kim learned to swim while recovering from a kind

of cancer that began to develop when she was still just a fetus growing in her mom's womb. After Kim had the operation to remove a tumor the size of a baseball from the right side of her chest, her doctor suggested swimming as a good strengthening exercise .

Role model, savior, and survivor: Kim has proven a shining example of them all!

Fighting Ignorance and Ignoring Obstacles

"Are you afraid of dying?" a boy once asked Ryan White.

"No," he replied. "If I were worried about dying, I'd die. I'm not afraid. I'm just not ready yet."

He was just a little boy from Kokomo, Indiana, when he was diagnosed in 1984 with Acquired Immunodeficiency Syndrome, or AIDS. Ryan got AIDS because he had hemophilia, a condition that doesn't allow your blood to clot, so he needed lots of blood transfusions from other people. People didn't know much about the disease back then, and many thought wrongly that they could catch AIDS just from being in the same room with someone who had it, or from touching something the person with AIDS—or something from his or her body—had touched.

Ryan put up with townsfolk saying he was going around to supermarkets and spitting on vegetables out of spite, and classmates at his middle school spray-painting horrible messages on his locker. But when school officials said he couldn't attend class, well, that was the last straw.

He and his mom sued the school for his right to an education and an end to the bigotry. This made life in Kokomo even worse and finally, when a bullet was shot through their living room window, they moved to a town called Cicero, where the townsfolk took them in as if they were family. In the process, Ryan grew up in the public eye, speaking softly and eloquently about a disease for which there was no cure. He taught kids that what's most important is how they live their lives that counts, not how they die.

"We'll all die someday," he always said. "Things could always be worse."

Ryan White did die, but not before helping to educate the world about this mysterious new affliction.

LOST IN THE JUNGLE

Noris Villarreal was flying home from a summer vacation to her tiny village in the Amazon jungle when the plane she was riding in began to drop quickly. The pilot told everyone to throw everything they could out of the windows to make the plane lighter. Noris followed the pilot's instructions.

The eleven-year-old Venezuelan, who was about to begin sixth grade, kept only a backpack with bread, canned deviled ham, and a Bible with which to pray as the pilot attempted an emergency landing in the remote river. Noris awoke several hours later to a nightmare. Three of the seven people aboard were already dead. With her broken wrist, she rinsed off one woman's face and fed a man bread and water as she tried to bandage his mangled leg with rain-soaked gauze. The survivors patiently waited for rescue.

Over the next two weeks, Noris's faith and strength would be challenged. Two badly injured passengers died, but the girl and another passenger who wasn't too badly injured managed to survive on plants. They prayed, while battling with hunger and biting bugs and mosquitoes. Still, these two survivors never lost hope that help would come—and it did. When rescuers brought them out of the jungle, people marveled that the two were still alive.

Noris wasn't. "The dead people didn't make me afraid, because God was with me," she said. "I felt him close."

Speaking Out

At age seven, Seth Green told his speech therapist that he wanted to be a politician when he grew up. She hesitated. "Why not try a less visible occupation?" she suggested.

Instead, Seth, born with a cleft lip and palate—a condition where the lip, palate, and gum don't fuse together, making it hard to eat and talk—became a debate champion and a spokesperson for kids with facial abnormalities. "As I gained confidence, my speech problems went away," said the Coral Springs, Florida, teen.

Over the years, Seth had eight operations for his condition. He knew kids could be cruel, and felt bad when adults, who should have known better, averted their eyes. So Seth, along with friend Emily Rose, began a group (ESTEAM for *E*mily and *S*eth's *team*) to help kids educate others about this. Then he helped with a Florida bill for insurance to do more for such kids.

Seth also spent time with hospitalized kids, fundraising for a hospital wing, and working for Habitat for Humanity.

Shark Bait
Fights Back

లనులనులనులనులనులనులనులన

His friends call him "Shark Bait," but Aaron Perez is really lucky to be around for them to call him anything at all. The eleven-year-old from Freeport, Texas, was wading hip-deep in a school of speckled trout at a local beach when he was attacked by a bull shark that didn't want to let him go. It came at him once, chomped at him, backed off, then it came right back again—hard.

Fortunately, Aaron had watched a series of shark programs on the Discovery Channel the week before. Even with the shark's sharp teeth embedded in his arm, Aaron kept his cool and remembered how to fight the thing off: He punched it in the gills really hard.

The shark finally gave up on Aaron and swam off when the boy's dad and a friend joined the battle, hitting the shark with the poles of their fishing rods.

While Aaron waited for a helicopter to transport him to a hospital, he asked those nearby to pray for him. At the hospital, doctors spent more than four hours reconstructing his shredded right arm. Aaron pulled through the surgery okay.

Now back in school, Aaron is glad to report that he has regained almost full use of his hand and is playing the violin again. He says he has no hard feelings toward the shark that nearly killed him. After all, the predator was only doing what came naturally—kind of like the family dog, Canaan, actually. Aaron knows not to mess with Canaan when he's eating!

Aaron still likes to go fishing with his dad, although now they stay snug in a boat, which suits this young fisherman just fine. It could be said of Aaron: Once bitten, twice shy . . . and alive to tell the story.

No Quitting

Once Amanda Stewart had been a high school track star, basketball player, and cheerleader. She was a popular kid who never thought about death and dying; she was way too young for that. In just a few seconds—the time it took for a car she was riding in to run off the road and roll over—the way she looked at the world changed.

She was only fifteen when the accident happened, which made her paralyzed from the waist down. However, she didn't let this get her down and came back from lengthy hospital stays without having lost her outgoing nature and the drive that had first made her a leader in her school in Keyes, Oklahoma. Not being able to walk, well, that was that, and she just had to deal with it. Her motto: "Winners never quit, and quitters never win."

Amanda began talking to students across three states about the dangers they needed to think about the moment they got into a car, whether as a driver or passenger. As a representative of Oklahoma's Think First program, she talked to groups of students, making them see that drinking and driving didn't mix. Getting into a car, she said, is a great responsibility. It's important to take it seriously and always take the time to fasten your seatbelt.

Her message shook some kids up, maybe because she wasn't an adult telling them what to do, but one of their own, sitting in a wheelchair. There were times when tough, broad-shouldered football players left the room crying.

Amanda's work didn't go unnoticed in the larger world, either. She was one of nine American students in her age group (out of 5,000 applicants) to be awarded university scholarships worth $20,000 each. In order to win, she had to maintain at least a B-minus grade point average, and demonstrate accomplishment in at least four of five categories: leadership, obstacles overcome, unique endeavors, special talents, and community service.

Amanda also did really well in a sixth category not measured on the application: courage.

❧ 4 ❧
HELPING HANDS

DO YOU LIKE TO HELP OUT? ARE YOU ONE WHO LEAPS UP WITHOUT PROMPTING AND SAYS, "DON'T WORRY, MOM AND DAD, I'LL CLEAR THE TABLE AND TAKE OUT THE GARBAGE"? NO? IT'S OKAY. THE KIDS IN THIS CHAPTER ARE PROBABLY NOT LIKE THAT, EITHER. BUT THEY ALL HELP OUT IN BIGGER WAYS, WHETHER IT'S WITH FOSTER KIDS OR THOSE WHO ARE HUNGRY OR HOMELESS OR SICK CHILDREN OR PETS.

HELPING KIDS COPE

Sometimes Sasha Bowers woke up not knowing where she was. Sometimes she was so tired and hungry, she couldn't focus on her schoolwork and practically fell asleep in class.

This was the result of being homeless and having to hop from one shelter to another from the time she was five. The honor-roll student kept hoping that things would change.

When she, her little sister, and their mom finally moved into a two-bedroom apartment in Columbus, Ohio, Sasha, fourteen, couldn't forget the kids still in the shelters. She felt for these kids who had to sleep in different places each night, fight off bugs and hunger, and toss and turn on hard cots as the cries and snores of other people kept them awake.

Sasha knew that staying positive meant being busy and having fun, so she got the Youth Empowerment Program, a state group representing the disadvantaged, to help her set up a summer day camp for more than 250 homeless kids.

At Columbus's Franklin Park Conservatory, the kids can experience some magic, spending their days planting flowers, weeding, fishing, reading, and playing. "We can't blame ourselves or our families for not having a roof over our heads or enough food in our bellies," Sasha explained.

Sasha's work won't stop there, either. When she grows up, she wants to be a lawyer who helps families find shelter and improve their standards of living.

Seeking Excess Baggage

Many kids wouldn't pay much attention to what a big sister's complaints about her work. Aubyn Burnside and her little brother, Welland, were different. When their sister, a social worker, complained that foster kids she worked with had to put their stuff in big plastic garbage bags when they traveled from one home to the other, these kids paid attention.

Only nine and seven at the time, Aubyn and Welland listened back in 1997 as their sister asked their mom to donate suitcases from the attic. They decided to start their own drive. For the first two weeks, they diligently checked the boxes they'd placed outside of churches and post boxes in Murrells Inlet, South Carolina, but no matter how much they wished and prayed, there was nary a suitcase given. Finally, their mom said, "All right. You guys tried hard, so how about I take you to the store and buy you thirty suitcases?"

As soon as their mother bought the suitcases, other donations came flying in from all over the region. Big bags, little bags, medium-sized bags—there were so many that Aubyn and Welland thought it was like a miracle. So began Suitcases For Kids, which now operates across the U.S. and beyond, complete with six regional vice-presidents.

"We sure don't sit around a lot," said Welland with a grin. "It's kind of neat and scary that people like us could start this kind of project."

Aubyn, who just entered college and dreams of writing books for children, says one of the hardest parts of running the show was public speaking, not so much to adults but rather to people her own age. "I can't help but feel that they're thinking, 'Like, man, she's a geek.'"

Helping others isn't the sign of a geek; it's the mark of a good person—in this case, two.

KiDPaCkS
WiTH a PuRPoSe

When David Adamiec saw one of his best buddies carrying a familiar blue backpack for abused or neglected children, he was shocked. He knew that bag as if it was his own, but he had no idea that his friend was having problems at home.

"Gosh, what do you say?" he asked. "Actually, I didn't say anything. I don't want to embarrass him."

This is David's life and what he calls his mission through God. The Westbrook, Connecticut, teenager was twelve when he began what is now a nonprofit organization called Kid Packs of America. It provides underprivileged kids with bags filled with five days' worth of clothes, toiletries, and games. The school bags come equipped with notebooks, pencils, and pens. It has even provided bags and packs to kids in Haiti, Venezuela, Afghanistan, and Iraq.

Because he wants to protect their privacy, David doesn't get the names of the kids he prepares packs for. Instead, he finds out their age, gender, and clothing sizes through conversations with grown-ups like school principals and nurses.

Sometimes it's hard being David's age, with adults saying things like, "My, but you act so maturely!" The way he figures it, if he can change their minds about teenagers in general, then the rest doesn't matter.

Texas Toy Box

Lauren Bothwell isn't sure exactly what made her do it. Maybe it was when her dad, a doctor, took her to the local hospital as he made his rounds and she saw lots of sick kids who looked sad. Or maybe it was because she knew she was lucky to live in a comfortable home and have as many toys, books, and videos as she wanted, while other kids didn't.

Whatever it was, something sparked in Lauren when she was eight years old that made her determined to hold the best toy drive ever in Harlingen, Texas. She thought there were other kids out there who would also want to help. So she sent out 650 notes to the students at her elementary school. The note asked them to bring in toys for children who were in the hospital because of illness or injury. Next she set up a drop-off box in school.

Lauren was both surprised and delighted with the results. That first year, she collected more than 1,000 toys, books, and videos, and made a homemade thank-you pin for each kid who donated something. Since then, she has established "Lauren's Toy Box" as an official enterprise that collects and distributes toys to children who are hospitalized.

"The kids are real kind, and it makes me really kind," Lauren says. "There was a little girl named Vanessa and she was just so thankful and happy for the toy I gave her—a Barbie—and it makes me feel good to be able to do that."

She Talks
To The Animals

Maybe it was the expressions in the animals' eyes, so melting and gentle, they seemed full of tears. They didn't have a home like she did, a place where they were wanted and loved. The first time Meagan Sokol of Uniontown, Pennsylvania, saw a newspaper ad asking for dog food to feed abandoned pets at the Fayette Friends of Animals Shelter, she was determined to work there every free moment she had.

Soon the twelve-year-old was cleaning out foul-smelling kennels, telling part-time shelter employees what to do, and talking to the animals as if she'd been doing it all her life. Terriers, pit bulls, poodles, tabby cats—it didn't matter. They'd crowd around as she told stories and assured them that someone was going to take them in and love them as much as she did. "No way that your owners gave you up because they didn't like you," she told them. "Just something in their lives made it hard for them to keep you."

Meagan could find the good in anyone and anything. She used that good in the profiles she wrote about the animals for the shelter's quarterly newsletter. "Meagan's Picks" were more than just "loving dog needs good home" notices. She filled the pages with quirky details and observations that turned these creatures from unwanted animals into living, breathing beings; for example, Benny, a year-old black lab mix, loved to play and be cuddled like a baby on car rides. He looked forward to these mini trips because at the end he knew he'd get a scoop of vanilla ice cream at Vinny's Ice Cream Parlor—maybe even in a cone!

Shelter board member Cheryl Qualters, who nominated her for a volunteerism award, says that Meagan's mind never quit working for the animals. Every single day she had off, she made sure that it was spent at the shelter. She had become such a big part of operations that it was easy to forget just how young she was.

"Meagan's family were those animals," Cheryl said. "I don't want to cry, but she's like Dr. Doolittle. The animals all adapted to Meagan beautifully." Meagan won a $5,000 scholarship from a national department store for her good work. When she grows up, she wants to be a veterinarian. Of course!

Weighing In

Some nights, Kimberly Greenwood couldn't sleep. She sat up thinking about kids just like her going to bed hungry. She read newspapers and magazines, and she saw documentaries about famine, about families both far away and in her home state of New Hampshire not having enough to eat. Only twelve, she already knew about the side effects of starvation, the distended bellies, rotting teeth, and worse.

Kimberly wasn't one to stand back and do nothing. So she organized a "Hunger Awareness Week" at her middle school in Portsmouth, both to educate other kids and to raise money to feed people in need. It wasn't easy planning something to catch and keep the attention of adolescents. "I had to come up with activities that get people to have fun while learning about hunger at the same time," she said.

The collection drive she started brought in 1,269 cans of food that went to a local food bank. A raffle, food fast, bake sale, and a "dress-down pass," kids could buy to wear regular clothes that day instead of the school uniform, brought in more than $750 for local and international charities.

One of her more interesting and creative ideas was to take wasted cafeteria food—stuff like soggy French fries and half-eaten grilled cheese sandwiches—and weigh it right in front of the students. It was a graphic way to show how much they were tossing in the garbage without a thought.

COMPUTERS FOR KIDS

When Elizabeth Scoville began elementary school, only half the adults in Kentucky's Laurel County over the age of twenty-five had even graduated from high school, while only eight percent had earned a college degree. These weren't good statistics, and Elizabeth wanted to help change that.

Gradually the thirteen-year-old realized that new technology would help. But how could she get computers into people's homes? They were expensive!

The Y2K scare, in 1999 was the answer to her wish, with lots of businesses buying new computers. Many businesses she contacted were happy to donate their old machines to "Computers for Kids." Elizabeth learned how to reformat hard drives, install programs, and fix hardware. Each time she got a computer ready, she'd meet with staff from her school to select just the right child to receive it.

One little girl said, "I wished upon a star and my wish came true."

THe TuRKey ExPeRTs

Siblings Dan and Betsy Nally like to talk turkey—and lots of it. It all began one night before Thanksgiving 1996, when they were horrified by a TV news story about a shortage of turkeys at the Greater Boston Food Bank.

Dan was nine at the time, and Betsy was just six, but that didn't stop them from having a serious discussion with their parents. The thought that people would have to go without a Thanksgiving turkey seemed wrong to them, but what could they do? There was a frozen turkey in their freezer that the family didn't really need. Couldn't they donate that?

If the Nally's had a spare turkey, maybe other families

did too. So the kids went door to door in their neighborhood in Westwood, Massachusetts, asking people to donate whatever turkeys they had in their freezer. The Nally family loaded the family Jeep with thirty-six frozen turkeys and drove into town to deliver them. Sure, the birds were hard as bowling balls and couldn't be handed out until the following week—but it was the thought that counted. After that, plans for their turkey drive got bigger and better.

For a few years they delivered hundreds of turkeys in a U-Haul, which was so heavy that the bottom of the carrier actually scraped the pavement. Then they made the switch over to giant refrigerated trucks.

Nine years later, Dan and Betsy have become turkey magnates, having turned their holiday food giveaway into Turkeys 4 America, a nonprofit organization, that last year gave away about a million turkeys across several states! As young as they are, these two kids have become experts in everything from federal nonprofit filings and haggling over turkey prices to getting out the word in classrooms and challenging fellow students to help feed the hungry.

How did they grow to have such big hearts? Their parents, Cathy and John, taught them well—and their dad's sudden death from a heart attack a few years ago made them redouble their efforts to keep his name and teachings alive.

THE POWER OF A BEAUTIFUL WORD

In the Mohawk language, "skawenniio" means "beautiful word." Skawenniio Barnes took this to heart. A scholarship student from the Kahnawake reserve south of Montreal, Quebec, she'd always dreamed of a cozy library near her home where she could curl up with a book after school.

When the thirteen-year-old Canadian closed her eyes, she could imagine it: a whitewashed clapboard house, with hundreds, maybe even thousands of books inside, especially those with Harry Potter, the boy wizard who can do anything if only he sets his mind to it.

Skawenniio just *loved* Harry Potter; he was such a hero.

What to do? Skawenniio's mom laughed. "Go make some of your own magic," she said. So Skawenniio wrote a letter to Kahnawake's community council about the "dire" need for a library and got involved in a fundraising committee. Then on the spur of the moment, she entered an essay contest for *CosmoGirl!* magazine about her dream of building a library. She wound up winning the contest and was named the magazine's girl of the year, complete with a photo shoot at the Strand Bookstore in New York!

"All those books, well, it was . . . awesome," she said, fondly remembering the photo shoot. Then another really awesome thing happened as well.

Books poured in from donors all around the world from places as far away as Australia and Germany. There were travel books, picture books, grown-up novels, encyclopedias and, of course, several sets of the Harry Potter series by J. K. Rowling, of which Skawenniio was such a big fan.

In October 2003, Skawenniio proudly cut the ribbon at Kahnawake Library's official opening ceremony in a former fire hall. The magic worked—thanks to a devoted girl who worked hard to make her dream a reality.

~5~
LIGHTS! CAMERA! ARTISTIC EXPRESSION!

THEY DANCE, SING THE BLUES, PLAY INSTRUMENTS, DRAW, AND EVEN DIRECT FILMS. THESE KIDS ARE ACCOMPLISHED BEFORE THEIR TIME IN ALL SORTS OF WAYS—THOUGH IT WASN'T ALWAYS EASY. THIS GOES TO SHOW THAT HARD WORK AND PERSEVERANCE CAN SOME-TIMES HELP FIND THE ARTIST IN YOU!

FOLKLORICO, OLÉ!

History and dance have always been very important to Chrissy Padilla. So it was only natural that she'd combine the two when, at age ten, she chose to create a community service project as part of a school assignment.

She started the International Ballet Folklorico at Horace Mann Elementary in Glendale, California. Folklorico was a traditional dance troupe for kids who came from poorer economic backgrounds and spent much of their time without supervision because their parents weren't home.

This after-school activity not only gave them a chance to have fun, but the dancing helped to teach the kids about their culture and make them proud of their heritage. The girls swished their big, lacy skirts as if they'd stepped straight out of a fiesta in Mexico, while the boys click-clacked in their heels and acted regal, graceful, and gallant.

The project had real staying power. For years, Chrissy choreographed and trained the kids, raised money to buy costumes, sewed capes from material like old brocade drapes she found in a store, and repaired and dyed donated shoes for kids who couldn't afford to buy their own.

She was a whirlwind with a mission, who led practices for up to 200 kids for an hour each Friday throughout the school year, giving them hope, inspiration, and pride. *Olé!*

Healing Notes

ᘓᘔᘓᘔᘓᘔᘓᘔᘓᘔᘓᘔᘓᘔ

When he grows up, Jourdan Urbach wants to be a neurosurgeon. Until then, the Roslyn, New York, teenager will have to make do as published novelist, philanthropist, and concert violinist who made his debut at New York City's prestigious Lincoln Center at age eleven. Oh, and once, when he was performing for severely brain-damaged children, the doctors came running when something—maybe the notes he coaxed from his violin—literally moved a little girl who'd never before responded to anything around her.

Call him a renaissance boy, with his long, sensitive fingers in lots of different projects. He began to play violin when he was two, and he's written two books, the first a science-fiction novel. His latest work, *Inside the Music*, is a fictional look at the lives of students at a music school that sounds a lot like New York City's Juilliard.

The book's first line is a question: "Where does fame begin?" For Jourdan, it began when he was just a toddler of twenty-two months. He loved music and could name the notes of anything. He heard melodies just about everywhere, even in the whistle of the tea kettle, the beep of a horn, or the whirr of the vacuum cleaner.

There was more to Jourdan though, than just talent. While still in grade school, he started a charity called Children Helping Children, in which young musicians give concerts throughout the New York area to benefit pediatric hospital wards. He got the idea after meeting a pediatric neurosurgeon while doing research for a school project on the brain. He knew the healing power of music, and he also knows that healing is what he wants to do for the rest of his life so it seemed only natural to combine the two.

When he made his first appearance on the main stage of Carnegie Hall in January 2005, he wasn't just performing in one of the most renowned concert halls in the world, he was performing to help others. The proceeds from this event went to charity, with the Long Island chapter of the Multiple Sclerosis Society and the National Pediatric Multiple Sclerosis Center at Stony Brook University Hospital getting needed money for their programs.

"I'm making a difference," he once said, "in whatever little way I can." This young musician is definately playing his part in trying to make a better world for others.

THE BLUESMAN

Nathan Cavaleri was three when he picked up a ukulele and began to coax sounds out of the strings. A year later, he was playing outside his mom's café near Sydney, Australia.

By age six he had leukemia and needed chemotherapy. He told the Starlight Foundation, which turns the wishes of sick kids into reality, that he wanted to meet and jam with Mark Knopfler of the rock group Dire Straits. "Done," came the reply. He flew to London and played guitar with Knopfler, who couldn't believe the young man's talent.

Though thin and weakened from all his treatments, Nathan still blew away the older musician with his natural blues feeling and fire—and he continued to impress.

Close your eyes to listen, and Nathan sounds like someone much older who's lived the blues. "That kid, he must be somebody reborn," the late blues master Albert Collins remarked after playing with Nathan, then nine, at the 1992 San Francisco Blues Festival. "He's got fire or something."

By thirteen, he was touring with the likes of blues legend BB King, had released a CD, and had his music featured on the sound track of the Disney film *Camp Nowhere*. He even had a tiny role, playing a nerdy kid who suddenly becomes totally cool when he picks up a guitar and starts to play!

He's not a kid anymore. He has recorded two albums and has his own grown-up sound. Totally cool.

GReaT Scott!

At age five, when most kids think about what's on TV, Gregory Scott was planning what he'd make for them to watch. The youngest-ever professional director was a kindergartner in Tarzana, California, when producer Al Burton saw him in 1991 on a TV talk show, showing home videos he'd made with his pet dogs and some school buddies.

"He was like a [university] film student," Burton said. "The only difference was that he was five years old and vertically challenged." Gregory loved the spotlight, too. Even though he was still learning to read and write, he got to meet people like director Steven Spielberg and give lots of interviews. Of course, everybody asked him why grown-up actors would listen to him. " 'Cause if they don't do what I say, they know they're out!" he replied, showing he had the instincts for this tough business.

His first official directing gig had him direct kid's entertainer Gregg Russell during part of a one-hour TV special. "I'm thrilled to get to work for such a smart little guy," Gregg said. Well, why not? Lights . . . camera . . . action!

THe Comics Kid

Sakura Christmas has been drawing ever since she can remember. Caricatures, portraits, and images seem to flow directly from her mind. She can even take the unseen and make it into a work of art, like the time she drew what she thought the deep ocean's floor looked like.

When her dad got her and her little sister, Mari, the dog of their dreams, Sakura began to draw her new basset hound, too. Nana, whom they rescued from a North Carolina animal shelter, had personality to spare, and Sakura wanted to capture that. Out of Sakura's doodles became a comic strip based on what she imagined was Nana's somewhat self-serving and always amusing advice.

She called the strip "BAD Advice from Bagnana," because basset hounds have skin that falls in baggy folds. When she showed it around, many people thought it was good enough to take down to the local newspaper, the *Durham Herald-Sun*. So she did, and the strip ran for years, from the time Sakura was twelve to when she left Carrboro, North Carolina, the town where she grew up, to start her freshman year at Harvard University!

Bagnana was known for quoting (and often mangling) famous lines, such as the Oscar Wilde one: "I can resist everything except temptation." The strip was syndicated across the country, and Sakura began another cartoon, a more sophisticated single-panel drawing she called "Laissez Faire," a French expression that means "Let It Be." This became her second syndicated cartoon.

How did she do it? Well, Sakura says a big factor was that she and her sister grew up without a TV at home. Since she can't play computer games to save her life, she doesn't waste time trying. That left a lot of time for drawing.

Her parents, who were with the Peace Corps, encouraged their daughters to use their imaginations, so the girls listened to classical music, created plays, and drew constantly. "We were artistic, dramatic, actress-type children," said Sakura, whose name is Japanese for "cherry blossom."

ACCORDIaN PRODiGY

When you think of the accordion, do old-fashioned polkas and monkeys come to mind? Now meet Cory Pesaturo, who makes playing an accordion look positively cool. Really.

The teenager from Cumberland, Rhode Island, has been playing ever since he was small. He started playing because his father did, and with the help of teacher Tulio Gasperini, himself a legend in the accordion world, Cory soon played better than his dad. Soon he had gone on to win the U.S. Piano Accordion Championships.

Sure, Cory does entertain at places like the local corned beef-and-cabbage dinner for senior citizens, but he's also made five appearances at the White House, where he once got the Clinton family and then–Hungarian president Arpad Gonez to tap their feet to tunes like the "Beer Barrel Polka"!

At Cory's own high school graduation in June 2004, he played "Tico, Tico," a super-fast, technically difficult piece of music. This got everybody in the room whooping, hollering and, finally, rising to give him a standing ovation.

Cory bowed, then stood there like a rock star, his finger pointing skyward.

Pig Performance

Mirror, mirror on the wall, what's the fairest sound of all? Kaitlyn Filippini loves to spend time in her family's bathroom, but not to fiddle with her makeup. Instead, she fiddles with the 121-year-old German violin that she calls "Pig."

The acoustics in the bathroom are the best, she thinks—better, even, than the state-of-the-art music studio her parents built for her in the basement! The sound bounces off the tiled walls in a way that allows her to really hear the notes.

Kaitlyn should know because she's been playing the violin since she was nine. She even has her own violin performance business, Eloquent Acoustics. This young lady has become such an accomplished performer that she hires herself out to play at events such as weddings. She performs with an orchestra at the University of Nebraska in Omaha and twice joined rocker Rod Stewart on stage as a violinist for concerts in Omaha and Kansas City, Missouri!

She got *that* gig through a referral. She was more excited than nervous, even though she only got to practice the music once before playing it for real. "The curtain went up and everybody was screaming," she said. "It was so great."

What's that? A violinist who plays Mozart calling a Rod Stewart concert great? "You can handle only so much classical music, so you balance it with rock," she said.

A Flute Player's Mouth

When she was young, Brittany Vogt hated smiling because she was convinced her teeth and jaw were the ugliest things in the world. Then, one day, her seventh-grade music teacher in Jonesborough, Tennessee, told her that she had a mouth that was made to play the flute.

When she went home that afternoon, she was smiling so wide, her face seemed like it was going to split. "Mom," she said, "I have the mouth of a flute player."

So began Brittany's love affair with music. Even through braces, which she wore for what seemed like forever, and the painful jaw surgery she had in her sophomore year of high school, the flute kept her grounded and focused. Music made her grow. It challenged her and lifted her when she was down, and she never stopped being amazed by the fact she was creating beautiful sounds by blowing into a metal pipe.

Wanting to share the magic with kids less fortunate or more isolated, she began to teach children how to play the flute at her local Boys & Girls Club. Soon she realized that volunteering a few hours a week wouldn't be enough. School budget cutbacks left little money for after-school activities, and funding for instruments was one of the first things to go. Instead of giving up, Brittany came up with a plan.

The response to her lessons at the Boys & Girls Club was tremendous. More kids than Brittany could ever have handled on her own clamored to learn clarinet and trumpet. She asked for help from her school band teacher, but realized they needed outside help, so she learned how to write grants and knock on doors to ask for money.

She organized both a benefit concert and an auction and in the end, she had enough volunteer tutors, money, and donated instruments to go ahead with her plan.

Since then, Brittany's program has been such a success, she's designed a how-to manual for other Boys & Girls Clubs. She's even looking to expand it across the U.S.!

Hear Her Song

Ashley Gearing's biological father died from a brain tumor when she was only nine months old. She always wondered what he was like, and maybe she poured some of that feeling into the song, "Can You Hear Me When I Talk to You?"

In June 2003, three weeks after her twelfth birthday, the song debuted on *Billboard*'s country singles chart, making her the youngest female singer ever on the country charts!

The song touched a chord. People called in requests to radio stations across the country, from Los Angeles to Nashville and her hometown of Springfield, Massachusetts. They wanted to hear that plaintive golden voice singthe song of a child talking to her dead father.

The buzz around her led to a bidding war (she signed with Disney's Lyric Street Records). Since then, she has recorded, performed in concert, and sang "God Bless America" at a 2004 Red Sox–Yankees playoff game.

It's sure a long way from Ashley's first public performance at age six, when she sang "A Spoonful of Sugar" at a music recital. Her music certainly goes down smooth—and sounds oh so sweet.

Voice of Experience

One writer described Susan May Wiltrakis's three-and-a-half-octave voice as that of an older woman—a woman who had lived a long hard life and seemed to have had her heart broken quite a few times.

Everybody who knew Susan thought this writer's description was pretty funny. You see, the thing is that Susan was all of twelve at the time. Already a seasoned performer, she crooned and acted under the stage name "Susan May." She was also enough of a tween to love hanging out at the mall near her home in St. John, Indiana, not far from the city of Chicago, Illinois. Child performers can, in one moment, speak—or sing—of hearts broken and lost love, and in the next, talk happily of their latest find at the Gap.

Susan started young. She began dancing at age three and singing at six. She started acting in a repertory theatre at nine, and a year later became the youngest-ever member of the Chicago Cabaret Professionals. Then when she appeared on Oprah's talk show to promote her CD, *The Rose*, well, she just blew the host and audience away with her vocals!

These days, she's working more on finding the right balance between school, a social life, and performing. Eventually, she'd like to go into medicine, but that will be down the road a bit. Right now, she can't wait until she turns sixteen, because then she'll finally be able to drive herself to gigs.

6

MEDIA MOGULS AND SPORTS STARS

THEY'RE DRIVEN. THEY HAVE VISION . . . THESE ATHLETES ALSO HAVE TERRIFIC HAND-EYE COORDINATION. IF YOU'VE EVER TRIED TO HIT A GOLF BALL OR EVEN PLAYED A VIDEO GAME, YOU'LL KNOW WHAT THIS MEANS! THESE KIDS HAVE TASTED BOTH FAME AND SUCCESS AT A YOUNG AGE, DISPLAYING PERSEVERANCE THAT MANY PEOPLE EVEN TWICE THEIR AGE HAVE NOT BEEN ABLE TO MUSTER.

Speaking to the Stars

ᔕᑕᔕᑕᔕᑕᔕᑕᔕᑕᑕᔕᑕ

Fred Medill speaks to the stars—Hollywood stars, that is. The Beverly Hills, California, teen has had his own Web site, called FredTV, since he was twelve, and also hosts a premium channel movie news show for ages eight through sixteen. He's at every local red-carpet event, asking actors like Nicole Kidman and Tom Hanks questions!

At the premiere of *Me, Myself & Irene* in 2000, for example, Fred asked Jim Carrey: "What kind of research do you do to play a man suffering from advanced delusionary schizophrenia with involuntary narcissistic rage?" He was fourteen then—Fred, that is, not Jim Carrey.

FredTV began as a way to entertain hospitalized kids using mobile computers. This program was called PC Pals and sponsored by the Starlight Children's Foundation, an organization that makes life better for ill children. Fred liked to make the kids smile. So when his dad got Fred a press pass so he could interview Adam Sandler at the premiere of *Big Daddy*, Fred took the mike and ran with it.

He hasn't forgotten the Starlight kids, either, having over the years invited a number of them and their families to come along and meet favorite celebrities. He knows how to provide red-carpet treatment to both stars and Starlight kids.

WeLL UNDeR PaR

Morgan Pressel made history in 2001 when she became the youngest golfer ever to qualify for the U.S. Women's Open Championship. All of twelve years old at the time, she had a blonde ponytail, braces on her teeth, and a whole lot of dedication to a game that she has been practicing at least four hours a day. She spends plenty of time on her studies, too, though. Math is her best subject, although adding up her low scores isn't all that challenging.

This girl from Boca Raton, Florida, managed to qualify for the U.S. Women's Open even before she was eligible to play in an American Junior Golf tournament! She could drive the golf ball really far—even farther than some of her more experienced competitors.

Although her score was higher than the prescribed "cut" to play in the final two days of the tournament, this young newcomer was still one of the most watched players at the U.S. Women's Open at Pine Needles Golf Club in Southern Pines, North Carolina.

Practice, Morgan knew, was good for both the stroke and the soul. It was an escape from all the hype—the media requests for interviews and kid groupies who all clamored for her autograph. *Her* autograph. Why, only five months earlier, Morgan had been among these young fans, standing in line to get famous golfers to give her *their* autographs.

Young Feet

To say that running a marathon is hard is quite an understatement. Completing a 26.2-mile course is one of the hardest things a typical grown-up can ever do. Some will end up walking. Others will just quit. Imagine the surprise when spectators saw Taylor Robbins running past them in the Suzuki Rock 'n' Roll Marathon in San Diego, California!

"Hey, little man!" they shouted out to the twelve-year-old runner. He waved to the crowd with a raised hand, but he didn't let their offers of food, water, and Gatorade break his concentration. It took him five hours, four minutes, and four seconds to cross the finish line, and afterwards, he was a changed boy.

"I just feel different," he said, "like I can pretty much do whatever I want, if I put my mind to it."

The Second
Coming of Oprah

She has talked to singer India.Arie about the pressures of growing up different. She has spoken to tennis stars Serena and Venus Williams about sibling rivalry and the mental steeliness they need to master their sport.

As the founder and publisher of *Blackgirl* magazine, Kenya Jordana James of Atlanta, Georgia, is certainly not short on mental steel herself. After all, she started the bi-monthly publication when she was only twelve years old, using $1,200 she'd made selling homemade cakes!

Kenya decided there was a need for *Blackgirl* because she couldn't find a publication that spoke to her interests as an African American curious about everything from black history and culture to entertainment and style. "Go ahead," said her mom. So she did—and now, the magazine, which is geared toward girls ages twelve to sixteen, has 5,000 subscribers, and is sold in bookstores across the country.

Plainly put, *Blackgirl* is interesting. You can find articles about hip-hop in South Africa as well as homeless teens, book reviews, and even stories and poems submitted from readers. Best of all, it's not saccharine sweet and unrealistic, like so many of the publications marketed to teens.

"Empowerment" is Kenya's motto. She was named

Black Enterprise magazine's Teenpreneur of the year, and she has appeared on BET, CNN Headline News, and, of course, *Oprah*. Kenya and Oprah, who publishes her own magazine as part of her media empire, bonded immediately. They shared their experiences on TV about how it can sometimes be a drag finding advertising!

Kenya isn't going to stop there, though, not by a long shot. She likes coming up with ideas and turning them into businesses—and she's quite good at it. Recently she began to sew clothing that she designed herself, which she plans to sell to her friends for starters. Called Modest Apparel, it's the kind of fashion that treads the line between cutting edge and "Approved by Mom" because it's not too tight or too short. Like Kenya, it's just right.

BLACKGIRL

PiNG-PONG WiZaRD

Once Darius Knight liked to hang out in the playground near his home in a very poor part of London, England. His friends were there, after all, and a basketball hoop and a bunch of other things kept the ten-year-old interested. When a coach convinced him to take up Ping-Pong, though, he picked up a paddle and never looked back.

He practiced all the time in a large garden shed that doubled as a clubhouse for the Ping-Pong players. There was room for only one table. It was heated by a wood stove in winter. In the summer, it got as hot as a sauna.

It didn't matter to Darius. His moves were lightning quick, even in the cramped space.  Just a mere two years after he first took up the sport, he took the Ping-Pong world by storm, winning the under-12 event at a European championship! "I adore playing the game," he once said. "It's taking me all over Europe, and I really believe that, if I have the right attitude, I can become the best."

Informed and Intelligent

Jason Crowe knows how to make a difference. Instead of sitting around and moping when he found out that his beloved grandmother was diagnosed with cancer, the nine-year-old from Newburgh, Indiana, had the idea of starting a kids' newspaper to raise money for cancer research.

Written by and for kids, *The Informer* dealt with tough and important subjects such as racial unity, global warming, persecution, and religious tolerance. It also taught its readers how to raise money for charity! He donated the profits from the newspaper sales to the American Cancer Society.

Jason's interest in world news led him to another project that touched him. The year after he founded the newspaper, he read about a cellist in Sarajevo, Bosnia, playing for twenty-two straight days in his homeland in memory of twenty-two men, women, and children killed by a mortar shell that fell among them while they stood in line for bread. The cellist thought art should bear witness to tragedy, and Jason agreed. So he organized a concert with twenty-one cellists and one empty chair, on which sat twenty-two roses in a vase. This became the start for the non-profit The Cello Cries On, Inc., an organization devoted to bringing peace to the world.

～7～
THE GIFT OF GIVING

THE OLD SAYING GOES THAT IT'S BETTER TO GIVE THAN IT IS TO RECEIVE, BUT IT'S NOT ALWAYS THAT EASY. IMAGINE GIVING UP YOUR BIRTHDAY GIFTS! IT WOULD BE HARD, WOULDN'T IT? WELL, ALL THE KIDS IN THIS CHAPTER HAVE GIVEN UP THEIR PRESENTS OR FAMILY KEEPSAKES OR ALL THEIR SPARE TIME TO HELP OTHERS—WITHOUT THE EXPECTATION OF GETTING ANYTHING IN RETURN . . . EXCEPT FOR THE SATISFACTION OF DOING GOOD.

A HaRD CLiMB

Why did Erica Estey give up getting presents for her ninth birthday? Well, she loves climbing almost more than anything else, except maybe for ice cream, skiing, and, *okay*, basketball. The money that would have gone for gifts was put toward buying a $10,000 climbing wall for her elementary school's new gym in Kensington, New Hampshire.

Besides, the $210 given on her behalf to the wall fund set such a fine example that donations flooded in. The school's jump rope team contributed, as did Grades 1, 2, and 3. Erica's little sister, Casey, also chipped in. A fund in memory of local athlete David Barrows, who died many years earlier in a car accident in Utah, donated $2,000.

Two years later, a pre-made wall has finally been bought and delivered. Erica can't wait. Once it's up, she wants to be the first to the top, if only to show how it's done. After all, she began to rock climb at age seven, when her birthday party had a climbing wall.

"They thought they'd fall," she says. "They didn't know how to use a harness so they wouldn't take a tumble."

And she hopes that people will think of her whenever they look at the wall in Kensington School's gym. "I want them to remember me because I'm a crazy kook-ball and because I started it all," she says. "It'll be a fantastic challenge for kids and there is no better present than that, right?"

Pitching In

ᴜᴄ∩ᴜᴄ∩ᴜᴄ∩ᴜᴄ∩ᴜᴄ∩ᴄ∩ᴜᴄ∩

Thomas Fortner doesn't live on a farm but he sees and reads enough to know that being a farmer is not an easy life. Even so, when his neighbor, farmer Rodger White, lost his arm in an accident, the boy from Taylorsville, North Carolina, pitched in to help. "I don't know why," the boy says. "I just wanted to. I want to be a person who helps other people when I grow up."

Then eleven years old, young Thomas had never worked a farm before, but he set his mind to it and that was all there was to it. Every day after school, and even on weekends, you'd find him there. With farmer White to guide him, he worked in the chicken house, grading eggs and cleaning out the coop. He also fed the cows, mowed the lawn, pitched hay, learned how to drive a tractor, and generally did everything that White used to do before his injury. Sure, it was really hard to learn all the things he needed to know, but Thomas gave his all and never gave up.

What happened to be his favorite chores? "Well, driving the tractor was pretty much a lot of fun, and putting out hay and feeding the cows, that was the best. They're really smelly, but you get used to that and they're so big and funny," Thomas stated with a smile.

A nice bonus for Thomas was the $5,000 scholarship he won for his good work through a program sponsored by

Kohl's department stores in the U.S. A teacher at his school had been impressed with his efforts and nominated him, and he's still very aw-shucks about it.

"It's all well and fine, but Mr. White just needed help is all," he says.

Rodger White, though, is not aw-shucks about it in the least. After all, when times were at their toughest, Thomas was there for him instead of off playing baseball or skateboarding or doing whatever else kids do these days. Thomas has made himself a friend for life.

"He is a wonderful young man," Roger White said admiringly. "He took the place of my right arm."

85

A GOOD WISH

At first glance, Elizabeth Roten's eighth birthday party in Springfield, Tennessee, looked like a really good time. It took place on a big farm, with pony rides and a pig to pet. The kids played badminton and croquet, and then came a big cake in the shape of a horse .

The difference was that when it came time to go home, Elizabeth didn't take any gifts with her because there weren't supposed to be any. After her birthday the year before, when she got so many presents she didn't know what to do with them, Elizabeth had decided that she wanted all her guests to bring some kind of a donation in her honor for the Make-A-Wish Foundation of Middle Tennessee. At the end of the day, more than $400 had been collected!

Elizabeth, who's crazy about horses and just started karate classes, learned about the foundation from a flyer that her mom, Ruth, gave her. The stories about children who were fighting deadly illnesses such as cancer—children who could have been just like her—really touched her heart. Some of these kids had so little, and she had so much. So she told her parents that she wanted to help these sick children.

"These people do great things for these kids," Elizabeth said. "I just thought that last year I got a ton of presents and I don't need that many presents, so I thought, 'Why not give money to Make-A-Wish?' "

A Gust of Energy

Cara Ronzetti knows what hurricanes are like. After all, she lives in South Miami, Florida, which was hit by four of them in 2004. Besides Ivan, Frances, and Jeanne, ten-year-old Cara will never forget Hurricane Charley. That storm, which landed on August 13, caused severe damage, but a friend of one of her teachers lost her home and everything in it.

The friend and her husband were expecting a baby in just a couple of weeks and had worked hard preparing the house for their firstborn. And Cara thought she could help.

Cara went home and asked her dad to get the family crib down from the attic. This crib had been used by no fewer than three children and had even survived 1992's devastating Hurricane Andrew, with winds up to 177 miles an hour!

Cara took the crib apart and prepared and packaged it for the soon-to-be parents. Then she and her mom took it to her school for pick-up. A crib couldn't replace everything, but it did give the couple something they needed and showed that their child would come into a world where even strangers go out of their way to help.

৩ 8 ৩
BEYOND BORDERS

FOR MANY KIDS AROUND THE WORLD, SIMPLY MAKING IT FROM DAY TO DAY TAKES SUPERHUMAN EFFORT. LISTEN TO WIVINA BELMONTE, WHO TRAVELS TO A LOT OF THIRD WORLD COUNTRIES AS PART OF HER JOB WITH THE UNITED NATIONS CHILDREN'S FUND: "THE STRANGE THING IS THAT SIMPLE 'SURVIVAL,' IN TERMS OF THEIR DAILY LIVES, IS NEITHER SIMPLE NOR ORDINARY. INDEED, IT IS OFTEN EXTRAORDINARY."

An Eye For an Eye

Growing up in Houston, Texas, Priti Dangayach heard about how her great-grandfather, a playright who lived for words, was going blind and only regained his sight thanks to generous members of his community in India. The long-time Girl Scout decided it was time to return the favor!

But how do you return a favor that involved giving sight back to one who lived for the written word? Simple: All by herself, the seventeen-year-old organized a three-day eye clinic in India. Girl Scout leaders privately expressed doubt that she wanted to do the impossible. The logistics! It would be hard to get even one doctor involved!

In six months of planning, Priti got *twenty* doctors and nurses to the village of Nawalgarh, in Rajistan in northeast India. The residents in the area suffer from serious eye problems due to the sun's ultraviolet rays, combined with lots of dust, a poor diet, and limited access to medical care.

Plus, Priti pulled together a great local publicity campaign, which included information pamphlets and a van equipped with loudspeakers to spread the word of the free eye clinic over a hundred-mile range.

In all, her team of medical experts saw more than 700 patients, many of them suffering from cataracts, just like her great-grandfather. No less than thirty operations were performed each of the three days of the clinic.

GiRL PoweR

Sahanatou Abdou stood straight and showed no fear as she faced the audience of elders and peers in her village in Niger, Africa. "We, the girls of this region, ask our parents to not give us in marriage at an early age and to not arrange marriages for us," the fourteen-year-old stated.

For a long moment, the audience was silent. Such a bold statement was unheard of, and especially from a girl! This was a real break from tradition. It was revolution. After

all, girls in the country of Niger had always married early, sometimes even as young as age twelve, and nobody had seemed to have a problem with it before. Half the girls in Niger are already married and have their first child by the time they had reached the age of sixteen.

However, Sahanatou felt that this life was not for her. She had dreams and goals that didn't involve leaving school and having children while she was still one herself. Just because this had always been the way things had been didn't mean that things couldn't change. In fact, things were changing. There were new laws, and she knew she had rights. Why, she'd heard about a father in another village who'd been arrested for arranging the marriage of his young daughter!

Sahanatou was brave enough to try to change what had gone on for as long as people could remember. Happily, her statement was greeted with support from one of the committee of elders. "The girls are right," he told the people gathered for the meeting. "If this is what they expect from us, we'll go along with them. From now on, none of the girls in our villages will be given in marriage before the age of seventeen or eighteen, and no girl will be forced into marriage."

Her brave words in the face of tradition helped make the lives of young women throughout Niger better—not to mention improving Sahanatou's own life.

Carry That Weight

Neco Kunga didn't look like he'd be able to carry the heavy generator across the border from Angola to Namibia. His shoulders were too narrow, and his knees buckled.

However, eleven-year-old Neco waved off help because he didn't want to split the thirty kwanzas, or about forty cents, he'd be paid for the delivery. He needed the money to buy a wheelchair for his disabled father. This boy is only one of nearly three million Angolan children whose lives were turned upside down during a civil war that lasted nearly thirty years. Now there is widespread poverty, a ruined education system, and shattered social services. One in four children dies before the age of five.

The surviving children are often on their own or, like Neco, have the difficult task of caring for their parents. "Some days I wake up and think things will be better today, but on other days, I don't want to wake up at all," he said.

But Neco does wake up, and he goes out and tries to make things better for his family.

"We Are all The Same"

This was Nkosi Johnson's motto: "Do all you can with what you have, in the time you have, in the place you are."

Nkosi lived that motto until the day he died. He was twelve years old and had suffered a great deal. Born in a nameless shantytown in South Africa to a mother with the disease, he entered the world already infected with HIV, the virus linked to AIDS. He was one of millions who had been infected in a country where the government had denied there was even a problem.

When Nkosi spoke from his heart about the disease's toll, people seemed to sit up and take notice. "Care for us and accept us. We are all human beings, we are normal. We have hands, we have feet, we can walk, we can talk, we have needs just like everyone else. Don't be afraid of us," he told an audience of thousands at the International AIDS Conference in Durban, South Africa, in 2000. "We are all the same."

The last line of his speech there became the title of a book about him. Later that year, he told an AIDS conference in Atlanta, Georgia, "It is sad to see so many sick people. I wish everyone in the world could be well." This thin, thoughtful, and brave kid became the symbol of his country's AIDS crisis, and he will never be forgotten.

FReeiNG CHiLDReN

It was just a photograph of a twelve-year-old boy in a bright red vest, with his clenched fist held high in the air, but it changed Craig Kielberger's life forever.

It was 1995, and Craig was twelve, the same age as the boy in the picture. One morning, as he was getting ready to go to school in Thornhill, Ontario, he grabbed the local newspaper to check out the comics page, but a photo on the front page caught his eye. He read the photo's caption, and it stopped him in his tracks.

The boy, Iqbal Masih of Pakistan, had been four when his parents sold him to pay off a debt. He worked as a carpet weaver twelve hours a day, six days a week, crouching as he tied tiny knots in the rugs. When he spoke out in protest against this situation, he was killed.

Craig was shocked. Before, he had never even known that child labor existed and now, he couldn't forget that there were 250 million other kids out there like Iqbal. He decided he had to do something to help them. But what?

Craig gathered some friends together, and they founded an organization called Free the Children. The idea was to stop child abuse and exploitation in every country. They also wanted to empower kids into thinking that they really could change the world if they just would make the effort.

They started with a letter-writing campaign to world

leaders. Then the kids set up information tables in public places, and Craig and the others spoke to students and other groups about their mission, and organized events like car washes and garage sales to raise money.

Six months after the Free the Children organization had started, Craig was invited to speak at a major union convention. He so impressed the delegates, they donated $150,000 for building a rehabilition and education center for kid laborers in Alwar, India!

Soon after that, Craig finally spent seven weeks traveling through Bangladesh, India, Thailand, Pakistan, and Nepal to meet the children he was fighting for. Since then, Free the Children has grown into an international network, with more than 100,000 kids helping each other in thirty-five countries—proving that nothing can stop you if you want to change the world.

If You'd Like To Learn More

Some of the kids in this book have joined or started really super organizations. Below is info to find out more about some of these worthy causes* so that you can help them or maybe even start a good cause of your very own!

Kids Who Care Pediatric and Cancer Fund
Web site: www.kidsthatcare.net
Email: ktckidsthatcare@aol.com
Kids That Care
7731 SW 62nd Ave, Suite 202
South Miami, FL 33143 USA

Youth Empowerment Program
A Program of the Coalition on Homelessness and Housing in Ohio (COHHIO)
Web site: www.cohhio.org
Email: cohhio@cohhio.org
Fax: 614.463.1060
COHHIO
35 East Gay Street, Suite 210
Columbus, Ohio 43215

Suitcases For Kids
Web site: www.suitcasesforkids.org
Suitcases For Kids
P. O. Box 1144
Hickory, NC 28603

Kid Packs of America
Web site: www.kidpacksusa.org
Email: david@kidpacksusa.org

Fayette Friends of Animals Shelter
Web site:
http://webpages.charter.net/ffoa/
Phone: 724.434.1422
Fayette Friends of Animals
P.O. Box 1282
Uniontown, PA 15401

Turkeys 4 America
Web site: www.turkeys4america.org
Email: turkeys4america@aol.com
Turkeys 4 America
P.O. Box 904
Westwood, MA 02090

BlackGirl magazine
Web site: www.blackgirl.com
Email:
editor@blackgirlmagazine.com
Phone: 404.762.0282
Fax: 404.762.0283
Blackgirl magazine
P.O. Box 90729
Atlanta, GA 30364

* Information was correct at press time; if your group or organization was featured in this book and contact info isn't listed, this is because up-to-date data was not available. Should you want to be included in future printings or editions of this book, please contact the publisher.

JUN 0 6 2007